50 Women: 50 Years

From the Ordinary
comes the Extraordinary

ISBN: 978-0-9932597-8-4

Commemorating 50 Years of Guyana's Independence

GOLDEN JUBILEE
OF INDEPENDENCE

GUYANA
1966 - 2016

INTRODUCTION

Somewhere in the early part of 2016 I decided to write a book about Guyanese women. I wanted it to raise the voices of Guyanese women and show the extraordinary things that ordinary women are doing.

My Guyanese-ness is a fundamental part of my identity. I remember the first day that I went to Primary School in Guyana at age 10, a boy got benched in front of me. I was horrified. They didn't beat children in London where I had been schooled previously and I was worried for my safety for weeks to come until I got used to the new rules and new way of being!

I have recounted that tale many times over the years with fondness and amusement because by the time I graduated from Queen's College in 1998, I saw nothing wrong with the corporal punishment we received and in hindsight found my reaction quite funny.

Throughout my adult life, I have found many likeminded Guyanese people who want to celebrate their rich heritage regardless of where they currently reside. Our conversations always centre around fond memories and I am alwas humbled by the great things that my fellow Guyanese, especially women, have achieved.

So, it seemed only natural that during this year,2016, which marks 50 years of independence for Guyana, I would publish a book capturing the memories, achievements and words of motivation and inspiration of some special Guyanese women. There are 50 main profiles in the book and motivation and wisdom from even more extraordinary women.

Through this journey I have also met many who wanted to make a positive contribution to Guyana but were not sure exactly how to. It was this desire that led to the establishment of Women of Kaieteur a Global Empowerment Network for Guyanese women and girls. Establishing the network has been one of my greatest achievements to date and I look forward to it going from strength to strength.

Finally, my advice to anyone reading this book is "don't ever let anyone diminish your contribution to the world around you. We all play a vital role in society and in life and you are as important as anyone else. There is no hierarchy in this game called life. Remember to live, love, listen, learn and laugh!"

Happy reading everyone!

Roianne C C Nedd

Women of Kaieteur – Chair and Co-Founder

FOREWORD

Thank you to Sherelle Cadogan, Women of Kaieteur Board Member who interviewed Mrs Thelma Lewis to provide the content for this foreword.

Name: Thelma Lewis MBE
Occupation: Retired medical scientific officer
Born: Bartica
Parents occupation: Father - postman, Mother -teacher

Aunty Thelma as Sherelle calls her told us that her earliest or most significant memory of Guyana was travelling around the country with her family because her father was a postman. She always had a bag packed to travel, in those days it was by train and she was always overwhelmed by the beauty of nature in her country.

She travelled from Parika to the islands and she also remembered the boat trip to Mackenzie aka Linden (from 8am to 4pm) which was always full of fun; music, food, drink and sometimes the odd woman dancing for money!

As she got older this specific boat would also bring over all the out of town boys who wanted to party in Georgetown! The joke would be if you didn't have a boyfriend before for that night you would sure enough get one.

Her **greatest achievements** to date include:
- Receiving a Certificate of Recognition for Charity work from the Guyana High Commission.
- A certificate of recognition and thanks from Pope John Paul II

- An MBE for charity work in 2005

Her charity work started when she visited Guyana following the death of her father. She visited the church and met the parishioners who had looked after her father in his time of need and she vowed to do her part immediately!

Upon her return to London, Aid to Guyanese was set up and for 32yrs she has sent 1 or 2 barrels home to the orphans and people suffering from leprosy every month. Aid to Guyanese remains the ONLY and most established group that supports these groups in Guyana.

We were also curious to hear Aunty Thelma's views about Women of Kaieteur and her response was positive *"Yes; this is a very important initiative for the women of Guyana. She told us that her mother was a teacher and always pushed education! She would say " You may marry successfully, you may marry unsuccessfully, you may have to run for your life, your husband's health may fail, you may never marry and through it, all EDUCATION will see you through!" She believes with education comes empowerment"*.

In terms of the greatest challenge for Guyanese women, Aunty Thelma felt that it was unemployment and we wholeheartedly agree which is why our initiatives include focus on employability skills and information.

Finally, we asked for words of inspiration to share with the network and our supporters. She said "Don't lose hope! Trust in God because without him we can't do anything".

We also wanted to share with you that Aunty Thelma is still finding new ways to help others. She manages a food bank; Manna as well as Spires which gives out underwear and socks to the homeless. This charitable nature was instilled in her by the influence of her parents, both were charitable with her mother sometimes giving away their shoes if other kids didn't have any and it was this upbringing that taught her not to cling onto things (possessions).

Contents

ALLISON LINDNER

Born: UK
Current location:
Canterbury, Kent, United
Kingdom

What is your earliest/most significant memory of Guyana?

I remember my time spent at Busy Bees play school in Georgetown quite vividly even though I would have been quite young. One enduring memory from my teenage years was my experience of camping over Easter in the Mazaruni with my family. I can still remember what it feels like to sit at the bottom of the waterfall before returning to eat the spoils of our daily fishing and hunting activities at our campsite.

What has been your greatest achievement?

Professionally, it has been being the recipient of a scholarship that is customarily given to about two dozen law postgraduates every year in the whole of the UK. I was also selected to perform in the Rio Handover segment of the London 2012 Olympics Closing Ceremony. As a South American, I felt really proud!

What words of inspiration/motivation do you have for other Guyanese women?

Keep working hard at whatever it is you want to achieve, so that when the right opportunity comes up, you are already prepared.

MELISSA YEARWOOD STEWART

Current location: Guyana

What is your earliest/most significant memory of Guyana?
Being part of the welcome chapter dance for the last held Mass Games

What has been your greatest achievement or proudest moment?
Graduating from law school

What words of advice would you give to other Guyanese women?
Though we are here to serve others, be true to yourself, desires and aspirations. Never compromise your moral beliefs, character and integrity!

ALTHEA B GARRAWAY

Born: Guyana
Current Location: USA

What is your earliest/most significant memory of Guyana?
My earliest memory of Guyana is living between Georgetown, and vacationing every year in a riverain community along the Demerara River. My maternal relatives were mainly located at Uitkomst village but in order to survive and make a livelihood, they had to interact with people from several villages, Dora, Warida and Endevour, to name a few.

The days passed with my cousins, and young aunts and uncles were most significant and formative in moulding me into a versatile "town" and "country-girl".

I learnt how to swim, catch fish, manage small boats, climb trees and walk through forest trails, to mention a few of the survivor skills I could not have acquired only from city life. To this day, those villages in that community area hold a place, dear to my heart. Oh, beautiful Guyana!

What has been your greatest achievement or proudest moment?
One of my greatest achievements was becoming a mother, studying for a graduate degree, while entering my first full-time job in a new country. It was an eye-opening experience into myself, mainly because it made me "see"

who I am and what I'm made of. There is a saying that "unless you're broken, you don't know what you're made of" and this rang true in so many ways. Many nights I did not sleep because of our grad school assignments, and I spent late afternoons planning lessons on the fly because I could not plan them at any other time.

My son tested all my boundaries and with patience running thin, I cried myself to sleep. I felt like I could not relate well to my students and probably seemed to be mostly angry. But through it all, God's grace kept me grounded, many times frustrated and bone-tired, but steady with hope that there was a silver lining behind the dark clouds of life.

My closest family and a few, close girlfriends (most of whom were miles away) strengthened me with advice, prayer, laughter, motivation and fighting grit. It was with new "eyes" that I saw how much I could endure as a woman, mother and teacher. Now, every time I face a new challenge, I remember the lessons I learnt in this process and use it as a catalyst to fuel my positive energies and dreams into joyful hope that "this too shall pass".

What words of advice would you give to other Guyanese women?

I would encourage my fellow Guyanese women to not lose sight of hopes and dreams, to seek out positive relationships because solid friendships are key to survival in life and to place trust in God. Just like nothing lasts forever, both negative and positive mould us into better persons, if we allow it to happen.

AVITA KARAMCHAN

Born: Guyana
Current location: USA/Guyana

What is your earliest/most significant memory of Guyana?
Absconding school to go swimming or hunting for birds, climbing trees, riding donkey, fishing

What has been your greatest achievement or proudest moment?
Supporting myself through college

What words of advice would you give to other Guyanese women?
Do not let a man's money influence you. Do not depend on anyone for anything. Being independent is the only way to be free

CHANDRALAKHA SINGH/RAMSINGH

Current location: Trinidad

What is your earliest/most significant memory of Guyana?
Life when L.F.S Burnham was President.

What has been your greatest achievement or proudest moment?
Proudest moment was when I recited one of my poems on open mike at the UPSCALE restaurant and bar in Stabroek, Georgetown, Guyana.

What words of advice would you give to other Guyanese women?
Strive to be happy and independent always

BARBARA THOMAS-HOLDER

(Senior Lecturer,
University of Guyana,
Faculty of Social Sciences)

Born: Guyana
Current location: Guyana

What is your earliest/most significant memory of Guyana?

My earliest most significant memory of Guyana is a humble upbringing in the country

in the early sixties. Rural Guyana was a beautiful place. I was born May 28, 1955 at Buxton Front and raised at Buxton/Friendship, East Coast Demerara, where everybody seemed to share the same common values of love, respect, religion, education, hard-work, family, community life and more. Every yard seemed self-sufficient with a kitchen garden and livestock and enhanced with a few decorative flower plants.

My grandfather, Papa Barnwell had farmland aback of the village and he brought home every conceivable fruit – mango, cashew, pear, soursop, limes, mamee, star-apple, guava, oranges, etc and all kinds of ground provisions including tanya, yams and dasheen. Every neighbour was an auntie or an uncle and everybody kept watch for the other regardless of race or creed.

As children, we played outdoor and indoor games including sal-out, pun-soo, hide and seek, jumbie lef he pipe ya, Jane and Louisa, snake and the ladder, ludo, jacks, Chinese rope, jump rope, and so many others. Afternoons and weekends used to be real togetherness; socialization that left such a wonderful taste in my mouth, with us also eating from any neighbour's pot. Then, in my head and in my own experience, race did not have a negative connotation. Yes, we were different, but so much alike. Life was beautiful! On school days, we would buy shave ice, mauby, pine drink, square cake, chip sugar cake and more with our pennies. We would share and really enjoy our differences - an Indian wedding or dig dutty, a negro queh, wake or funeral. I watched the Negro and Indian young men gambling under towering tamarind trees.

Can't forget this one – discipline – was ingrained because misbehaviour was not tolerated so a child was flogged for bad behaviour at home by parents or on the streets by elders or at school by teachers – no one escaped the ROD.

A different breed of people was raised then; times really changed! All this suddenly changed without any explanation to us children - 80% of the East Indians left the village within a wink, houses went up in flames, often we were sent home from school and told 'to run' till you reach home. British Soldiers were all over and families stayed off the road after a certain time.

The men in the neighbourhood would always congregate during the day and talk for what seemed like hours; "something was wrong" and those early days never came back after 1964.

In the countryside, we never really bought fruits as children, every kind of fruit was shared with us as the older folks would gave us what they accumulated in the baskets or calabashes. Our lunches were always shared with ten or more persons so we ended up with real 'dougla meals'.

Marriage and Deaths were real community events – the villagers gathered early to pick rice and cook outdoor with the wood fire. Ever since then we enjoyed smoked flavoured meals, thus Bar-B-Que isn't strange. Looking back, the nostalgia fills my mind. The overnight cook-up, the metemgee with salt fish and breadfruit, the chocolate tea with coconut milk on Sunday mornings, the weekend sweet bread, the boil egg for your birthday or rites of passage as a teen girl - the festivities where the food was brought in huge iron pots.

Lord, I miss those days! Days when we cooked daily, bought milk and ice daily and didn't have a fridge and microwave to store or warm food. Blackouts were many but we were accustomed to the dark and made good use of the moonlight and candles. We didn't have television or much household appliances to use electricity anyway. Those daily readings of a good book, listening to the radio and talking 'jumbie' stories under the moonlight were the best.

What has been your greatest achievement or proudest moment?

Even-though life changed, Education was and still is a cherished value. Now many local and foreign organizations support the village education drive. We all encourage and celebrate educational achievement within the village.

I, myself, have spent, to date, thirty-nine years in the field of education. My first stint was at Bladen Hall Multilateral School where I witnessed the commitment and warmth that drove the passion of teachers for the all-round development of their students. Followed by teaching English Language at President's College where we were a real family and the children found true parents even-though they lived away from home. In the early days, the first five years of President's College, our unity was unmatched and was so strong that even today, the bonds we made persist.

It's such a joy to meet and greet past students and teachers alike. The pride with which values were transferred has kept the flame alight. I'm a true country girl since my school and work life, was basically spent in the country except for a brief three years when I attended Lilian Dewar College of Education for Secondary Teachers (1974-1977). Apart from my job as a lecturer at the University of Guyana from the early 1990's to date, I have spent a significant part of my life working within communities especially with women and children.

My emphasis is mainly on informal education - social and moral development, understanding gender issues, self care, coping with social problems, building family relationships, improving income generation skills, embracing community history and more. Although I spend more time in my own community, I have worked in all regions of Guyana except regions 3 and 7.

My greatest achievement therefore is being a country woman who reflects honesty and integrity, spurns mediocracy and who has been able to raise a wonderful family, to nurture, touch and transform the lives of hundreds during the past four decades. I am a proud Buxtonian whose current residence is in Beterverwagting, an educator, wife and mother of four successful children and grandmother of six. God has been tremendously good and I will remain eternally grateful for the opportunities presented to be of service to others.

What words of advice would you give to other Guyanese women?
To other Guyanese women my advice is simple: Life's journey is never easy but do not let that prevent you from achieving your goals. Face your challenges with unwavering strength, pride and tenacity!

ELIZABETH CRITCHLOW REGIS

Current location: USA

What is your earliest/most significant memory of Guyana?
The area where I grew up Lodge Village on May Day the village Queen was crown and the platting of the May pole. I also remember girl guides and the outtings. My father took me to see horse race on Durban back Lands, these are some of my most significant memories.

What has been your greatest achievement or proudest moment?
My proudest moment was becoming a Registered nurse and midwife. On arrival in the USA, I was well equipped to work in any department at any hospital. I am very proud of my Nursing education in Guyana, it was a solid foundation that helped me to be successful in every area of my life. I continued my education and obtained a BSN and 2 Masters degrees, all built from that foundation.

What words of advice would you give to other Guyanese women?
Be focus, your life is in your hand, elevate yourself. Do not be happy where you are! always strive to do better and be better. Educate yourself, make sacrifices, have a business plan for yourself and never give up. Surround yourself with positive people and think only positive thoughts for your life.

BONITA ANDREA DOUGLAS

Born: Guyana
Current location: USA

What is your earliest/most significant memory of Guyana?
My most significant memory of Guyana; is me preparing to write the common entrance exams, as it was called back then. Having to complete your extra lessons homework for the next day under a candle light or kerosene lantern because we had "black- out" was normal for most students.

I don't know if kids today would have the motivation and drive to function under those conditions, but back then, this was the norm. You did what you had to do; looking back those are some of the sacrifices and life experiences that have set the foundation for my future achievement.

The late-night sacrifices paid off with me gaining a place at the distinguished Queen's College, this paved the way for my journey to adulthood and have moulded me into the hard working; dedicated person I am today.

What has been your greeatest achievement or proudest moment?
As a mother my greatest achievement has been my kids, for every one of them born, the instant joy, love and admiration I felt is indescribable and has gone down as

some of my proudest moments (as in yesss..I made this!). Knowing that I am not living for myself but someone else; who depends on me for everything; gives my life meaning and worth.

Aside from my kids my other greatest achievement has been completing my Master of Science in Global Business and Finance. Completing my masters was challenging for me because; it was as though I was juggling several jobs and wearing various hats.

Having a full-time job, taking care of three young kids, being a wife and studying could take a toll on anyone, I swore I never wanted to see another text book once it was over; but with perseverance the impossible is possible.

What words of advice and motivation would you give to other Guyanese women?
My advice to Guyanese women and some lessons I have learned along this journey call life would be; hard work pays off, keep dreaming, things may not happen when you want them to but they will happen when the time is right. I have learned that the universe has a way of giving you what you put out, positive thoughts and energy brings back the same.

Story of my life; as long as I can remember I have always wanted a job that would allow me to travel the world, this happened briefly when I was employed in Guyana as a Foreign Sales Representative. I migrated to the USA and it seemed as though I was never going to have that sort of job again, several years went by and I lost hope, but unexpectedly I was offered a position that not only allowed me to travel for work but also for leisure.

This is my testimony of never giving up on your dream, they will manifest when the time is right.

NEVLYN NICHOLSON

Current Location: Canada

What is your earliest/most significant memory of Guyana?
Growing up in Berbice surrounded by lots of fruit trees and never receiving any limits on when to stop picking and eating fruits.

What has been your greatest achievement or proudest moment?
Achieving my Executive Masters in Business Administration Degree (EMBA) in Barbados.

What words of advice would you give to other Guyanese women?
Share your experience and knowledge in a positive way

NICOLA LONDON

Current Location: USA

What is your earliest/most significant memory of Guyana?
High school being a part of the winning debate team for Queen's College the only girl on the team and in the same year being a part in the national championships and placing 3rd in javelin and 4th on high jump. This showed that you can be academically successful along with being athletically successful.

What has been your greatest achievement or proudest moment?
Becoming an OB/GYN, seeing how proud my mother was and then becoming successful in my field. Being named Baltimore top doctor by my peers for the past 5 years in a row.

What words of advice would you give to other Guyanese women?
Guyanese women are smart and adventurous. If you believe you can achieve. I was not the smartest girl in my class but I was determined to succeed and that is what has propelled me to where I am.

CAROL ALEXIS FRASER

Born: Guyana
Current Location: Guyana

What is your earliest/most significant memory of Guyana?
Grinding rice into flour to produce cake, buns, pasta and made fruits preserves from papaya. I always got A's in school for innovation.

What has been your greatest achievement or proudest moment?
When I was awarded first place and a gold medal in 2014 biannual Visual Art national Competition in the category of craft.

What words of advice would you give to other Guyanese women?
Make it your business to be or to create the wowwwwww...let your thoughts propel you to greatest.

SIOBHAN KENDALL-MORRIS

Born: UK

Current Location: England

What is your earliest/most significant memory of Guyana?

I have never physically been to Guyana but my experience of it is learning through my fathers childhood stories. He was a great story teller and he would transport me through his words.

What has been your greeatest achievement or proudest moment?

My greatest achievement has been raising a strong, educated accomplished young lady as a lone parent whilst completing my own education and building my career.

What words of advice and motivation would you give to other Guyanese women?

Take pride in your heritage and carry yourself with confidence and class as you navigate the many obstacles life throws at you. We can sometimes feel like it's an uphill struggle. One step forward and two back but this is what makes is strong. Persevere, above all never give up

CARLEEN BOLLERS

Born: Guyana
Current location: UK

What is your earliest/most significant memory of Guyana?
Independence celebrations when everyone was overjoyed at the prospect of no more colonial rule which was very significant in terms of the future development of our new nation.

Guyanese at home and abroad were unable to contain their excitement and for once there was unity among all the races which was in stark contrast to the civil unrest of earlier years which had led to mass migration. As a newly independent nation we were justifiably proud of not only the new name (signifying that links with the British had been relinquished) but also the unique design of our flag and rendition of our National Anthem, all of which instilled in everyone a renewed sense of pride while waiting in anticipation of the ceremony.

What has been your greatest achievement or proudest moment?
Volunteering with a government funded national telephone helpline for more than a decade offering emotional support to survivors of racially motivated hate crimes e.g., assault/verbal abuse/criminal damage, burglary, theft, sexual violence, harassment, bereavement by homicide and/or providing information at callers' request, regarding local/specialist services they could contact for additional help by appointment. On many occasions, callers would

choose to remain anonymous while talking through their various options particularly in domestic/sexual violence cases before deciding on the next steps, perhaps to report to police or seek legal advice. A key feature of the service was for staff to be empathetic, respect the individual's decision regardless of age, ethnicity, gender, religion or sexual orientation and to be non-judgemental.

What words of advice would you give to other Guyanese women?
Always follow your dream, challenge anyone who is disrespectful towards you/your family and remember the adage regarding all aspects of life - if you fail to prepare you prepare to fail.

DESA CALDER-GREENE

Current location: USA

What is your earliest/most significant memory of Guyana?
My earliest memory of Guyana is attending Stella Maris primary school. I vividly recall being surrounded by a new family away from home. Teachers like Miss Munroe, Miss Wyatt and Miss Lynette taught me discipline, respect, kindness and the value of hard work at a tender age.

What has been your greatest achievement or proudest moment?
My educational foundation in Guyana has yielded many achievements thus far. My greatest achievement to date has been passing the ever daunting NYS bar exam and attaining 10 years as a licensed attorney while working for a company I respect.

What words of advice would you give to other Guyanese women?
Never stop dreaming and growing. Embrace change and live life on your terms.

LORETTA EDWARDS

Born: Georgetown
Current Location: London

What is your earliest/most significant memory of Guyana?
As a child standing up at the rails at Durban Park watching the races. My other memory was also from my childhood. We went to live at Mocha Arcadia and I used to ride from Mocha to Central High School and I would tow my sister on the bicycle, there weren't many cars then!

What has been your greatest achievement or proudest moment?
My greatest achievement was adopting my son. Every day he has brought joy to my life and watching him graduate was one of the most special moments of my life.

What words of advice would you give to other Guyanese women?
Aspire to be the person that you always wanted to be and don't lose sight of that goal.

CAROL REID

Born: Guyana
Current location: UK

What is your earliest/most significant memory of Guyana?
My earliest memory is of a 4-year-old. There are not a lot of things I remember as a child. I remember the journey on the plane. I remember seeing my Grandparents for the first time and remember the back yard and having to walk over a plank as it was a bit muddy and my Mother did not want me to mess up my Sunday Best dress.

What has been your greatest achievement or proudest moment?
My proudest moment was attending my Dad's brother's funeral in Buxton. It was my first back home and I was overwhelmed by the attendance of what seemed like every adjoining village in the area. For the 9 night we had so many people come to show respect and talk of the love for my uncle.

My pride and joy was getting up to read in front of hundreds at the funeral and trying my best to speak as clear as possible. Even then some of my family could not make out my London accent lol. I love Guyana and my Uncle was always a helpful man in his community.

My dream is to set up a foundation one day for young women /girls in Guyana

What words of advice would you give to other Guyanese women?
Have no limits, be the best, love yourself first and everything else will come to place and you will shine.

EDNA ESTHER DOOKIE CRABBERE

Current location: England UK

What is your earliest/most significant memory of Guyana?

I was born, raised and received my early education in British Guiana, (now known as Guyana) South America, I am the 6th child of 12 children of Catherine and James Dookie – Citrus Farmers. My earliest memory is having fun on weekends with my family; eating peanuts while my daddy told us fairy tales and my mother singing for us.

What has been your greatest achievement or proudest moment?

When I achieved my University Degree for a publication called "Millennium Child 2000 Combo" (Genre- Early Education)" - I would have preferred for my parents to be alive to see that moment.

What words of advice would you give to other Guyanese women?

Take time out to search your heart; know who you are and do the work to reach for the sky because you are responsible for your own happiness.

DIANA BENJAMIN

Born: Mabaruma, North West District
Current location: Lincoln

What is your earliest/most significant memory of Guyana?

I grew up in a Catholic orphanage. Looking back now I think although I didn't grow up with my parents, the nuns tried their best to do what they had to do and in retrospect it was quite enjoyable. The life lessons that they taught me shaped my life and made me the person that I am today.

What has been your greatest achievement?

One of my greatest achievements is being a mother. My son has been my constant motivation and inspiration and through my journey as a mother I was able to build my self-confidence.

I used to be shy but know I am more confident because I know my own worth and value. This has helped me to find a job that I am passionate about. I work with people with disabilities which is very rewarding. I am lucky to be engaged in a field of work that I love.

What words of inspiration do you have for younger Guyanese women?

Believe in yourself. It is the key to everything and my own self-belief is what allowed me to finally unleash my self-confidence. I would also say that they need to see the best in every situation. Focus on the positives not the negatives.

EMILY SINGH

Born: Canada
Current location: Toronto, Ontario

What is your earliest/most significant memory of Guyana?
When I reflect on my memories of Guyana it is difficult to pick just a single memory that is the most significant to me.

However, I would say that my fondest memory of Guyana was when I was 16 years experiencing a speed boat ride through the mighty Essequibo River for the first time. I love the outdoors and one of the most beautiful things about Guyana is its untouched natural terrain.

I recall being so enthralled with the simple wooden construction of the boat yet so mesmerized by its ability to rip through the black waters with such power and force.

When it was finally our turn to get in the boat I was so excited yet so nervous at the same time. This memory, in particular, always stands out to be me because I could experience it with my dad, one of the most influential and most special people in my life. I remember looking over at him and seeing that same expression of excitement that he had when he would tell me stories about Guyana on his face as we speed through the river together towards Hogg Island.

What has been your greatest achievement?

My greatest achievement thus far would hands down have to be earning my Bachelor of Journalism Degree. When I reflect on those four years of study, I can safely say that education is truly the key to success. One of the greatest things about knowledge is our ability to use it to educate and inspire those around us.

Through my journalistic career I was blessed to be able to cross paths with people from all walks of life. As a journalist I was able to travel to India and report whilst meeting people who allowed me to tell their story. That is one thing that journalism has allowed me to do, tell stories while still adhering to a certain level of standards and ethics. This degree meant more than just the new-found title of "Journalist" it meant that I had successfully put my mind and heart into something and completed it.

The journey throughout my post-secondary education was much more valuable than the destination. I gained lifelong friendships and created memories that I will be able to reflect upon in the years to come.

What words of inspiration/motivation do you have for other Guyanese women?

First and foremost, I would inspire my fellow Guyanese women to believe in themselves and seek power, courage and ultimately strength from within. If you do not believe in your own unique abilities and talents no one else will. As women it is our duty to uplift, empower and motivate one another to the highest extent. In today's society is it so easy to get swept up in conforming to what society deems "beautiful". True beauty comes from one's character and is reflected in how they treat others.

Another piece of advice that I would offer to other Guyanese women is seek guidance and strength from God in all your endeavours. Whichever faith you follow put the Lord first in all that you set out to accomplish. When faced with trials and tribulations never let your trust and belief in God waiver, instead set your mind and heart into trying harder.

I would also say that surrounding yourself with a positive circle of friends is important in achieving your goals. Being around people who love you and want to see you succeed is so crucial especially when being faced with adversity.

That being said, I also want to remind my fellow Guyanese women that failure does not mean that you are not good enough it is simply a way of saying change your approach. One place that I often turn to for inspiration is the Bhagavad Gita, which is an ancient piece of Hindu literature. One quote in particular that speaks to me is as follows "Change is the law of the universe." When failures arise, we must look at it as opportunity to seek change whether that be in our approach, mind-set or attitude.

Lastly, I would tell my fellow beautiful Guyanese women to love themselves and always stay true to who they are and proudly represent their country and raise our golden arrowhead with utmost pride and remember that as Guyanese we are indeed "one people, one nation, one destiny."

MYRNA WILLABUS

Current location: USA

What is your earliest/most significant memory of Guyana?
The white sand, springs and valley of Wismar Hill.

What has been your greatest achievement or proudest moment?
My greatest achievement outside of knowing God, was the seven unpublished books I have written. They were delayed because of the noise of life, but now they are here. Look for the published books this summer. Blogger and business owner of www.playersgetplayed.com.

What words of advice would you give to other Guyanese women?
When you travel with honesty and integrity, nothing is unachievable. Straighten your spine and walk confidently

JASMAINE PAYNE

Current location:
Guyana

What is your earliest/most significant memory of Guyana?

I grew up in Guyana, so all my memories are of here. I have travelled to other places, but Guyana is home.

What has been your greatest achievement or proudest moment?

My greatest achievement thus far is being able to shed my fears and my hang-ups about following my dreams long enough to become a writer by profession. Growing up, I was told that just writing for a living was not something that that was practical. For a long time, I put my dreams of writing on the side burner and tried to fit into the expectations of what a 'practical, money making career' required, even trying to study Business instead of English at University. Finally, I decided to listen to my heart and I followed my passion.

Today, I write for a living, working as a freelance writer for the Guyana Chronicle and a Special Projects Officer at the Ministry of the Presidency in Guyana. I am editor for the Miss World Guyana Official Magazine, Majesty; I have also made contributions to 'Guyana at 50' - A book published by Hansib Publications in honour of our 50th Anniversary. I have my work published in an upcoming publication for Poetry and Jazz on a Stool. I just completed my BA in English at the University of London, and am also working on completing my first full length novel by the end of 2016. I have my own website www.missjazmania.com where I focus on featuring the Arts and endeavours of other passionate people like myself. I didn't want to live just to be practical, I wanted to live so that I could be happy and passionate about what I do. That way, whatever contribution I make to the world would be full of meaning because I put my all into it. I have much further to go in my writing career-

I plan on pursuing my Masters in Creative Writing in the near future, and to write several other novels if my life permits me. I may not be renowned, but I feel happy that I am living my truth and loving what I do! It feels so great every time I say 'I am a writer'. Life is good.

What words of advice would you give to other Guyanese women?
Follow your passion and never stop pursuing it. Do not compromise your dreams for anyone, let others fit in around your plans, not the other way around. Women must be fearless in their pursuits so that we can make the mark that we were always meant to make in this world. It is our time.

JOYCE SULLIVAN

Born: Guyana
Current location: Guyana

What is your earliest memory of Guyana?
My earliest memory of Guyana would be waking up to my Grandmother making 'toolsie tea' and having breakfast on the veranda. My grandmother would take these early morning moments to share her childhood memories with me and to educate me on the flora and fauna in the neighbourhood! I love those moments of humbleness and appreciation for nature. The beauty of Guyana.

What has been your greatest achievement or proudest moment?
My proudest moment was opening my own business in 2013. The Buttercup was the first flower my Grandmother showed to me and I can still remember thinking how simple and pretty it is. When I was thinking of names for my business, I wanted a name that spoke of strength and love. I opened Buttercup Day Care, Playgroup and After School Care. I am proud to be a part of a team that follows my strong principles and who love being Guyanese!

What words of advice would you give to other Guyanese women?

Believe in yourself, you are a strong and special woman and you can achieve any goal you have set. Be yourself. Be unique. Deal with yes and deal with no! Love and appreciate that you can make a positive impact in our beautiful country.

KEANNA MCLEOD

Current location:
United States

What is your earliest/most significant memory of Guyana?
My most significant memory of Guyana is visiting the sea wall. Here you have the Atlantic Ocean running over 200 miles along the coastline.

The water here is different. The land here is different. The water is different and with those things considered, the entire experience is different. Different in a good way.

Being there brings me to the feeling of what it means to be a Guyanese. Comparing American water and beaches to the sea wall in Guyana is truly not appropriate because there is nothing like it. It's a breath of fresh air.

What has been your greatest achievement or proudest moment?
My greatest achievement is being able to obtain a great education by way of a Bachelors and Masters degree. My mother was able to see me complete both so this made me even more proud of myself. Also, being able to manage numerous businesses has taught me a lot and has allowed

me to grow and progress to where I am now. For that, I am extremely proud and grateful.

What words of advice would you give to other Guyanese women?
Embrace who you are and where you come from. Embrace your womanhood and be independent. It teaches you a lot about self and self-worth. Success comes from within and starts with you. Take what you enjoy most or what your best at and take that craft and turn it into an achievement. Your happiness matters the most. If you find that you are unhappy in your life, what do you have to do to make yourself happy?

LEOTA MANGAL

Current location: Guyana

What is your earliest/most significant memory of Guyana?
Growing up in the country in a small village called Low Wood on the right bank of the Demerara River and helping my parents after school in the farm on the farm I will plant things like cassava, eddoes, plantain, bora and many more.

What I enjoyed on my father's farm was when I was hungry I would snack on things like roast cassava or plantain with butter or roasted corn. After leaving the farm you always saw my Dad with a string of bush fish.

What has been your greatest achievement or proudest moment?
Starting by own farming business at an early age.

What words of advice would you give to other Guyanese women?

To always believe in yourself.

LORI NARINE

Current location: USA

What is your earliest/most significant memory of Guyana?
My earliest most significant memory of Guyana is walking
to kindergarten with my father. I remember my father
gripping my hands tightly as we walked along the one-mile
stretch from my home to Glasgow Nursery School. We
would stop and talk to neighbours along the way and wave
at passers-by's. I can vividly remember meeting up with my
fellow classmates as we gathered in the school yard with
our matching uniforms, fancy lace socks, shiny shoes, and
cartoon character lunch boxes- which always contained a
flask of warm milk and some tasty snacks made by my
mom. This is my most favourite memory as it was the
beginning of my love affair with education.

**What has been your greatest achievement or proudest
moment?**
I am most proud of being a mom of two amazing children;
they give meaning and purpose to my life and this is what I
cherish most. My greatest accomplishment is the formation
of the SHEA Charity, because this charity has been, and will
continue to be a lifesaving portal for the underprivileged in
Guyana.

**What words of advice would you give to other Guyanese
women?**
Education is the key to independence and empowerment,
so my advice to Guyanese women would be to find your

independence, be empowered, be confident and never, ever pass on an opportunity to educate yourself. There is nothing sexier than a smart, independent, and liberated woman.

MALA BHEEM

Current location:
Great Britain

What is your earliest/most significant memory of Guyana?
Being allowed to play outside. Riding my bicycle everyone showing love and respect to one another. Going to 63 beach and going to the races.

What has been your greatest achievement or proudest moment?
Bringing up my daughters on my own. Watching them growing up to be amazing strong woman and don't let a man do to them What their father did to me. My proudest achievements being a grandmother and being able to help women and talk to them about domestic violence and being listen to. Sharing my experience in life to help others.

What words of advice would you give to other Guyanese women?

Be strong and stand up to what you believe in. Education is very important. You can lose everything in life but no can take away your education.

RAMONA NEDD

Born: Guyana
Current location: London

What is your earliest/most significant memory of Guyana?

I guess my most significant memory coming from my background was passing the 12+ examination to go to St. Roses. At that time, St. Roses was predominantly a school for people with money but here I was attending because I had worked for it. Often, I used to feel like I was in a crowd but yet alone at the same time. As if no one could see or hear me. I used to cry about it.

What has been your greatest achievement?

Achieving economic empowerment and independence was one of my greatest achievements. Being self-sufficient and being able to invest in property and have a successful career in the UK Civil Service before starting a successful childcare business.

What words of inspiration do you have for younger Guyanese women?

Be true to thyself" because unless you're honest with yourself then you can't achieve your full potential.

MALAIKA ARCHER nee CUMMINGS

Born: Georgetown

Current location: Canada

I like to sit and reflect on my life. It brings me so much peace. I've had a good life; my parents have done well for my siblings and me. They gave us what most parents without tons of wealth give their children; they gave us education.

You see both of my parents are trained teachers, so that education started from home and it was not just books, it was manners, etiquette, respect, you know the intangibles that are missing from the next generation. I take pleasure in passing on my life's lessons to my two children and it's nice when they display the intangibles, you feel a sense of accomplishment.

This overdue passage should be about me but I can't help making it about my parents. They are so entwined in me; I can't see a dividing line. I remember vaguely living in

Georgetown, in the first home my parents bought. When I think about it, my parents were just kids when they started out. Well kids in today's terms. They got married when they were 21 and 22. I was nowhere near marriage at that age. My dad a 22-year-old with a wife and a child. By age 32, I think they had all 5 of us.

At age 33 I feel overwhelmed with 2 and for some insane reason unknown to me, I want more. I can imagine the fear my dad must have felt at times knowing he had to provide for us, but he was a praying man, so as much as we grew up without a lot of tangibles we were happy and unaware.

My mom, oh my mom, the woman described in Proverbs 31: 10-31, this loyal, faithful, hardworking, provider. She knew her role and she _moved_ effortlessly daily completing her duties and tasks - Full time teacher, full time mother, full time wife, and full time gardener.

I have watched her for years and I don't think I will ever be half of the woman she is. My mom had us in order: she would shoot a sharp darting look with those soft light brown eyes and in that instant, you knew, yes you knew, the soft eyes were stern and then soft in that split second. In that split second the issue was resolved, a woman of few words but sharp darts.

What is your earliest/most significant memory of Guyana?
I remember growing up on the sugar estates; it was particularly fun when school closed and all the children in the compound would gather for games, bush cooks, raiding fruit trees, swimming and just having fun. We would be out

all day enjoying the sun, making go karts, having go kart races, taking sugar cane from punts as they passed on the way to the factory where sugar was made. Life was so simple back then.

(Malaika is in the red bow)

Well simple for us children because our parents carried the burden without complaint. I remember it was during the period of our history when the President wanted Guyanese to be self-sufficient and had placed a ban on certain food items. That forced my mom to get in touch with her green thumb, her inner farmer and every day we would tend to that garden, clearing, planting and reaping. I particularly liked digging for worms. We had chickens and ducks. It was the good life.

I am still friends with so many of the children that I met during that phase of my life. It was the good life.

What words of inspiration/motivation do you have for other Guyanese women?

- Have a personal relationship with your Creator, make Him the center of your life
- Practice positive affirmations daily, say what you want and if you eventually say it enough times you will subconsciously find yourself doing what you need to get it
- Find a partner who has common goals, that adds value to you
- Dream and dream big
  - Big dreams lead to big successes; small milestones are hit along the way that will provide satisfaction but small dreams cause one to fall short and give up
- Stay positive. Your positive energy will attract positive circumstances in your life.
  - Avoid negative people. It's easier for them to wear you down, than you to build them up
- Cut ties from toxic people that will try to kill your dreams
- Always have goals, always have a well-documented plan
  - Revisit and revise as needed, life is fluid, the tide changes
  - Be unreasonable with your goals, force yourself to move above the ceiling that you tend to set

- Think entrepreneurship, therein lies freedom of time and money
- Find something that you love doing, do it as often as you can, turn it into a business
- Do charitable work
- Self-improve daily

NICOLE RHONDA COLE

Current location: Guyana

What is your earliest/most significant memory of Guyana?

Mashramani Celebrations which is an Amerindian word that means 'Celebration after hard work'

What has been your greatest achievement or proudest moment?

The achievement of 'Independence' 50 years ago!

What words of advice would you give to other Guyanese women?

Be focused on your Career and work assiduously to better your Career prospects via 'Continuous Professional Development'! Strive for Excellence!

ROSELYN SHEPHERD

Current Location: UK

What is your earliest/most significant memory of Guyana?
Living in Guyana with my grandma who raised me. Life back then was hard but worth it. Made me appreciate who and what and where I am now!

What has been your greatest achievement or proudest moment?
Winning Miss Charlestown at secondary school because I wasn't the most popular girl so was delighted when I won.

What words of advice would you give to other Guyanese women?
Take care of family. Be a woman of worth. Conduct yourself like a lady. Demand respect.

MARJORIE GOMES

Current location: United States of America

What is your earliest/most significant memory of Guyana?
My earliest memory of Guyana includes performing in mass games and my dad taking me out to Home Stretch Avenue to see Muhammad Ali during his visit to Guyana.

What has been your greatest achievement or proudest moment?
I migrated to the United States of America in October of 2005 and began working as a Teacher's Aide in a Day Care Center almost immediately. I then enrolled in an adult education class in order to obtain a high school diploma. While attending, these classes the teacher, who was also Guyanese, suggested that I think about attending college.

After receiving my high school diploma, I enrolled in Medgar Evers College in January 2007 where I obtained my Associates in Teacher Education in June 2011. I then went on to obtain my Bachelor's Degree in Early Childhood Special Education in June 2013.

During my senior year at Medgar Evers College I was privileged to participate in a presentation presenting the process of lesson planning to an audience that included faculty, students and members of National Council for Accreditation of Teacher Education (NCATE). Members of the NCATE team were at the college conducting assessment for reaccreditation purposes and I considered this opportunity an honour to represent the college during this important process.

My greatest achievement yet was experience on June 1, 2016 when I graduated with a Masters in Early Childhood Literacy Education (birth- 6th grade) from Hunter College.

I am currently aspiring to get on board with the New York Mayor's Literacy initiative via literacy coaching with the New York State Department of Education and hoping that this come to fruition for the 2016/2017 school year.

In the meantime, I am working as the lead teacher in a Brooklyn Head Start early childhood program. In this my jubilee year (08/15/1966) I am proud to be able to say that I was born in what was a historic year for the beautiful nation of Guyana.

What words of advice would you give to other Guyanese women?
My advice to fellow women is that you must allow God to guide you, possess a vision of what you desire to become or achieve, "a must have mentality", a discipline and determination to leap over every hurdle that will pop up along the way to cloud your vision and see yourself

operating in your dreams even before they actually realized.

PATRICIA POMPEY-ROBERTS

Born: Guyana
Current location: New York

What is your earliest/most significant memory of Guyana?

I remember in my teenage years from 17 to 20 I really enjoyed having out with my friends and having a good time. I felt so free and easy. I used to play pool and explore Georgetown.

What has been your greatest achievement?

Being a mother to my husband's children and then taking care of the grandchildren has given me a lot of fulfilment as the family has grown I've enjoyed watching the girls turn into young women then mothers. Now I get the chance to do it in a more fun way with the grandchildren.

What words of inspiration do you have for younger Guyanese women?

Believe in your children. No matter what happens you must have belief in tour children even when others doubt them be there for them. Make them comfortable to talk to you. It's not just about being a parent be a friend as well be open with them and enable them to tell you their darkest secrets. This is how you empower them to avoid being abused and bullied. Replace their friends as their biggest confidante.

MAYLEEN MYRLEEN PATTERSON

Born: Guyana
Current location: Guyana

What is your earliest/most significant memory of Guyana?
My most significant memory of Guyana is being an Amerindian woman from the village of Santa Mission. I have had various experiences which motivated me to become a better person. The atmosphere of my community is one any individual would enjoy. The place is clean, beautiful and quiet.

What has been your greatest achievement or proudest moment?
My greatest achievement is having an education that will help me as an educator to help other people. Also, being a part of Women of Kaieteur 2016 strategy is an acheievement for me since I have a passion to help other women.

What words of advice would you give to other Guyanese women?
My words of inspiration/motivation for other guyanese women would be always be a strng and determined woman. Never give up on your drea because with God everything I spossible.

GENEVIEVE WITTER

Born: Guyana
Current location: UK

What is your earliest/most significant memory of Guyana?

After I left school I did two years at Carnegie and then in 1972 we had Carifesta which was a nice time and then I got a job as main cashier at Corrieas then two months later I moved to the St. Bernadette's Hostel on Lamaha Street.

The hostel was my happiest time in life. I enjoyed it. Then I worked at Kirpilani and Dasani then worked with Dr John Sawar as a receptionist

Why working at with Dr. Sawar I did a computer, accountancy and data processing course with Miss.Persaud in Waterloo Street, then I got a job at the Bank of Agriculture in Parade Street and then I came to Britain.

What has been your greatest achievement or proudest moment?

Having my son after I was told I wouldn't have children due to having cancer. It halted my life. When I found out I was pregnant I was worried because for five months they didn't know so when they told us, my husband and I stared at each other and I worried because I'd had all the treatment for cancer. I was worried for my unborn child. Then I was told that because there was no time for tests I could have an abortion but as a Catholic I couldn't sleep imagining what could go wrong.

So we decided to go ahead and we did the amniocentesis. A nurse followed up by saying that if I had a baby with Down's Syndrome I could have it adopted if it was too much for me. I couldn't believe what I was hearing.

I made a pact with the Lord that if my baby was born ok I wouldn't sue the hospital and now my baby has graduated from university

What words of advice would you give to other Guyanese women?
Don't give up in life and when you have good friends lean on them when you can. Don't give up. If you fall down get up. Every day is a new day. People are good out there, don't ever give up!

MONIQUE D KIRTON

Current location:
United States of America

What is your earliest/most significant memory of Guyana?
Going to Mackenzie High School in Linden, Guyana. I was somewhat of a under achiever just going to school to get an education. My friends were far and few. I remember that it was essential to wear one's full uniform or you will get spank or punish.

What has been your greatest achievement or proudest moment?
Today I'm proud to say that I'm the wife of Mr. Derek Kirton and mother of 2 handsome boys (Keanu and Kori Trellis) holding a MBA degree from Keller Graduate School of Management. I have a small business call Central Sporting Goods of New York Corporation and I'm also the Senior Project Manager for NY Department of Education managing their Lightower Conversion project. This project entails the implementation of high speed internet connecting into 1350 schools across the New York tri-state.

What words of advice would you give to other Guyanese women?

Never give up on your drive to achieve your goal. Take risks and always keep trying. Let no circumstances hold you down.

RUQAYYAH BOYER

Current Location: Guyana

What is your earliest/most significant memory of Guyana?
Fishing with the neighbourhood children in the black waters creeks of Linden, flying kites on the Hills nearby during the season of kite flying and Playing fun games of Sall- Out, Hop Scotch, and rounders after returning home from school every afternoon.

What has been your greatest achievement or proudest moment?

Apart from representing Guyana at the United Nations Peace Ceremony in 2013 at the UN Head Quarters in the United States. I would say winning the titles of Miss Guyana Universe 2012, Miss Guyana World 2013 and Miss Guyana International 2014 consecutively and thus being given the esteem opportunity to represent our beautiful nation on the international stage.

What words of advice would you give to other Guyanese women?
Don't live each day as if it's your last instead Live each day to chase your dreams. Work Hard, Stay Focused, Enjoy life and never settle for less than you deserve as a woman and as Guyanese.

SHANEZ RAMBHAROS

Current Location: United States of America

What is your earliest/most significant memory of Guyana?
I had to be about four years old playing marbles with my cousins in the street, while the glow from the setting sun dips into the horizon.

What has been your greatest achievement or proudest moment?
Getting my debut novel, My Rib, published. I was terrified to put my work out there, thinking nobody will buy it or nobody will like it. It was scary thinking that it wasn't good enough. Now I am a published author and I am glad and thankful for the push from friends and family.

What words of advice would you give to other Guyanese women?
Pursue your dreams. Don't be afraid to dream big and remember goals are made to be crushed.

LAURIAN BANCROFT

Born: Georgetown Guyana
Current location: Georgetown Guyana

What is your earliest/most significant memory of Guyana?
Funeral of L F S Burnham

What has been your greatest achievement?
My daughter. There is no greater accolade.

What words of inspiration/motivation do you have for other Guyanese women?
The only person responsible for you is you. So be accountable to yourself be ambitious for yourself be worthy of yourself and always be true to you

SHARON AUSTIN

Born: London, but was sent to Guyana as a baby...so that will always be "home" to me because my earliest memory is of Guyana
Current location: UK

What is your earliest/most significant memory of Guyana?
Love and care from my family, advice from my elders about getting the best out of my education and the vagaries of life and self-respect, excitement from each school day

What has been your greeeatest achievement or proudest moment?
Being able to work successfully and travel, as well as pass on some of my experience/knowledge to the younger generation to encourage them to try, to push for their goals

What words of advice would you give to other Guyanese women?
Homilies from my late, beloved grandmother: "After one time, it's another time", "You have to get up and get" and "If you don't try for yourself, no-one will do it for you".

SHARLENE PROFITT

Current Location: London

What is your earliest/most significant memory of Guyana?
Earliest memory was going to school on her own for the
first time at St. Stephens in Charlestown with my younger
sister and we got lost on the way home. We couldn't find
"BIG" (Stabroek) market, we walked down Princess Street
and ended up by the wharf because we missed the turning
and we asked for directions and people helped us

**What has been your greatest achievement or proudest
moment?**
My greatest achievement has been having my kids. They
make me happy and when I think about people who cant
have kids I feel really lucky.

**What words of advice would you give to other Guyanese
women?**
My inspirational words are work hard and aim for the
moon if you miss you may hit a start (W Clement Stone)
and if you fall down get up and go again.

SHERELLE CADOGAN

Born: UK
Current location: UK

What is your earliest/most significant memory of Guyana?
My earliest memory was travelling to Guyana when my
mum was pregnant with my younger brother in 1981, I was
5 years old. it was hot and I got chased by my relatives'
dog and fell and cut my face open. I had to go to hospital
and had an operation it was traumatic as the
anaesthetic didn't fully work. My dad held me down . I still
have the scar today

What has been your greeatest achievement or proudest moment?

My greatest achievement has been my children I became pregnant at 18 years old and my son is 21 years old. My second son is 9 years old and I am a lone parent. I have a great family, very proud of that

What words of advice and motivation would you give to other Guyanese women?

"– shine – just shine, never dim your light"

SHERRILYN MCPHERSON

Current location: USA

What is your earliest/most significant memory of Guyana?
My earliest and most significant memory of Guyana was a family vacation to Lethem. We stayed at a ranch style house with horses. I

remember these tall, clay ant nests that were so much taller than I was at the time and I was totally awed that ants could make something like that.

What has been your greeatest achievement or proudest moment?
Being newly immigrated from Guyana when I was 18 was such a challenging transition. Not only did I have to deal with understanding and fitting into a new placeand culture but I desperately missed my family and friends. Life in the USA has provided many challenges but also unique perspectives. This is truly the melting pot of many different cultures, people and foods. I am truly blessed for this humbling experience because it helped me grow as a person to not be so judgmental of others. Despite our differences our struggles are the same and that makes us the same …uniquely human.

What words of advice and motivation would you give to other Guyanese women?

Live life out loud. Be confident in your truth but be tolerant of other's diversities. Life is about learning, growing and being a positive influence maker. Let's get into the mind set of true sisterhood which is about supporting, encouraging and motivating each other. So, let's all strive to be phenomenal women.

TYRA

Current Location: Guyana

What is your earliest/most significant memory of Guyana?
I would say about when I was five years old. I lived not too far from the seawalls and I remember my father taking me and my siblings out there for a walk. I thought it was amazing, seeing all that water, just endless.

What has been your greatest achievement or proudest moment?
My proudest moment was probably on valentine's day, 2014. Instead of waiting for gifts from guys I spent the entire day baking and selling cupcakes. It was the first time I earned money on my own. It was a lot more fulfilling than chocolates and roses.

What words of advice would you give to other Guyanese women?
Embrace your womanhood and uplift each other. There are enough opposing forces trying to tear us down, we don't need to join in and contribute to that. We are the backbone of every society and we should never forget that.

SHIRENE PROFITT

Born: Guyana

Current Location: London

What is your earliest/most significant memory of Guyana?

My earliest memory is walking long distances to primary school and getting hit by a bicycle.

What has been your greeatest achievement or proudest moment?

My greatest achievement was getting a 2:1 in my BA Honours Degree in Business Management

What words of advice would you give to other Guyanese women?

My inspirationsl quote would be that anything is acheiveable with hard work and motivation. Independence is key, only depend on yourself and with strong will and inspiration you could achieve anything

YOLANDE C JULIEN

Current location: Nassau, The Bahamas

What is your earliest/most significant memory of Guyana?

So many memories, so little paper space. The question should be "50 of your earliest/most significant memories of Guyana". From kite flying on BV seawall every Easter Monday, to helping my dad make the actual kites using gamma cherry, to primary school days at St. Margaret's School (I remember every teacher in every class), to fun filled days at Bishops High School....it is endless.

I would say the most significant is Saturday afternoons at my grandfather and grandmother's house in BV. After Saturday chores at home, hair washed and combed in bubbles and slides (a Saturday routine done by my mom), my brother, sister and I would go to my grandmother's house to play and hang out with our other cousins who gathered there. My aunt made black pudding and souse to sell, so, we helped make it and then helped with the selling.

The best part of that process was making the sour for the black pudding, which sometimes ended up us having pickle mangoes. Thinking back now, we did so much in one afternoon, I feel now that time stood still for us as we had fun, but, back then, we felt like the time was too short. We never wanted to go home at the end of the night. My grandmother's yard was filled with every fruit tree...tamarind, mangoes, gooseberry dounce, guava, coconut, sapodilla and many more.

Our Saturdays was filled with eating fruits directly from the trees, salt and pepper in hand for the sour fruits. I have one vivid memory of me being the youngest and my cousins placed me in a comfortable spot in the tamarind tree with the pepper and salt and they were all in different parts of the tree picking, coming back to me for pepper and salt, and to give me mine to eat. Pickle mango, gooseberry, tamarind balls were a staple on those afternoons. I can go on and on with all that we did on those Saturday afternoons and the happy memories made there with my family.

What has been your greatest achievement?
Again, I can go on and on here. I have achieved quite a lot thus far in my life. Am thankful to God for the all. I would say my seamless pregnancy and the birth of Madyson my now 6-year-old "adult" is my greatest achievement thus far. It is a fascinating journey so far, with a lot of ups and downs. I am amazed at what is inherent in her and what is learnt. I look forward to many more adventures in parenthood.

What words of inspiration/motivation do you have for other Guyanese women?
My motto...I can do all things through Christ who strengthens me.

MICHELLE GRENADA

Current location: UK

What is your earliest/most significant memory of Guyana?
Born and bred in the UK, my earliest memories of Guyana
come from the stories my parents told me and my siblings
before I was able to go there myself years later.

What stands out is the apparent freedom my parents and
their peers had (after completing their chores and
schoolwork of course!) Everyone knew everybody and as
children of 'the village', the whole community looked out
for you. That also meant though, that if you got up to
anything you shouldn't be getting up to, it would be back
with your parents through the grapevine and you would be
looking licks!

The plentiful trees meant you could always climb a tree and
'fill ya belly' whilst on your adventures playing with your
friends. Before bed, at the weekend or after a celebration
sometimes the adults used to sit on the back step and tell
jumbie story.

As a child, being allowed to sit up with the adults made you
feel grown....until the elders told you it was time to go to
bed! Then you looked for any excuse to prolong not going
to bed whilst also trying not to reveal the real reason why!

When I first reached Guyana, I was struck by how friendly
everyone was. Walking by, whether you knew the passer-
by or not, the greeting was always, "Good Morning", "Good

Afternoon, or "Good Night". Most likely they knew you were related to someone in the neighbourhood and that you came from England on holiday to visit your relations! The native Guyanese could spot you a mile off! Was it the way I walked or looked?!!

It wouldn't be long before you were known by a 'nick name', as is customary with Guyanese tradition. If you said, wore or did something a little too often you would get stuck with that name - like Fish, Sugar, Night and Day, Buss' Rice, Salt Pork, Pumpkin, Hammer - and the list goes on! When the name sticks, if referred to by the individuals' given name - nobody knows them as that! The people are loving, friendly, welcoming and love to sport! Only in Guyana!

What has been your greatest achievement or proudest moment?

Life is a set of experiences, which accumulate over time. From the experiences, I have had it is hard to choose one particular time - however my greatest achievements and proudest moments are all around my abilities and what I have come through and my family ties.

For instance, I was proud when I put myself through post graduate study as much as I was proud to be the sister of one the greatest athletic performers of my school. Now, I am proud of my two sons, every day, and my oldest niece and nephew, who are just starting out in making a life for themselves.

What words of advice would you give to other Guyanese women?

1. Remember the importance of good family and friends around you. Good people are not just people who will tell you what you want to hear but those that will push, encourage you and support you.

2. Competition is not with others - it is with yourself - be better than you were yesterday.

3. You are unique - there are no 2 you's in the world. Find your strengths and talents and share them. Only you can do it in your own unique way.

4. Prioritise what you need to do and let everything else go. Trying to do too much results in either burn out or poor or little effort caused by spreading yourself too thin.

5. Help others whenever and wherever you can.

ROBIN F HAZEL

Current Location: USA

What is your earliest/most significant memory of Guyana?
There are so many memories. One of my early memories is spending Saturday afternoon at the Botanical Gardens with my family.

What has been your greatest achievement or proudest moment?
One of my proudest moments was standing up before the Florida Supreme Court to argue a case.

What words of advice would you give to other Guyanese women?
Find a network of support. Women helping women is a beautiful thing. Find that support for yourself and be that support for others. Whether you mentor the younger generation or just lend a listening ear to someone who needs it, the trajectory of your life, whether personal or professional, will be greatly improved.

PATRICIA CHARLES

Born: UK
Current location: UK

What is your earliest/most significant memory of Guyana?
Most significant memory of Guyana was when it became Independent from Britain

So much was happening at the time including visits by The Queen and Heads of States from various countries

What has been your greatest achievement or proudest moment?
My proudest moment was when the family businesses started and my greatest achievement was finishing High School and moving on to greater things in life

What words of advice would you give to other Guyanese women?
My advice to other Guyanese women is that they should put education first and climb the ladder to the highest level whilst holding their heads high with pride.

With education, the world will be their oyster and they must always reach for the stars. It is not impossible if they believe and have faith

SAMANTHA SHEOPRASHAD

Current Location: Guyana

What is your earliest/most significant memory of Guyana?
My earliest memory goes back to when I was 3 years old.

What has been your greatest achievement or proudest moment?
Attending Carifesta and the Golden Jubilee

What words of advice would you give to other Guyanese women?
A Guyanese woman is an asset to the world itself. You start by developing a clear, positive, exciting, and inspiring self-ideal, consistent with the very best person you can imagine yourself becoming.

You develop a positive self-image by imagining yourself performing at your very best in everything you do. Your self-esteem is the power source of your personality. It determines your levels of energy, enthusiasm, motivation, inspiration, and drive.

The more you like and respect yourself, the better you do at everything you attempt. And the better you do, the more you like and respect yourself. Self-esteem and personal excellence reinforce each other.

No matter how many setbacks or obstacles you experience, make the decision that you will keep on picking yourself up and persisting until you eventually succeed.

By deciding in advance that you will persist, no matter what the difficulty, you give yourself a psychological edge. Never Give up.

MAGGIE HARRIS

Current location: UK

What is your earliest/most significant memory of Guyana?
Falling out of the window age 2 and a half!

What has been your greatest achievement or proudest moment?
Winning the Guyana Prize for Literature twice, in 2000 and 2014, and Caribbean Winner of the Commonwealth Shirt Story Prize 2014

What words of advice would you give to other Guyanese women?
To believe you are a unique human being with your own special gift. There is not another like you. Whatever your race or creed you are an essential part of the human race. That you should believe in yourself and take every opportunity to better yourself. But in so doing, to do so in a holistic way that will benefit others. To support other women and encourage young people. Confidence comes with belief, in yourself and your aims, whatever you choose to do. I have used my work in education to inspire creativity, enlighten others about the diversity of rich Guyanese culture and history.

Sharon E. Sobers Stuart.
Current Location:
Fayetteville, Georgia.

What is your earliest/most significant memory of Guyana?
My most significant memory of Guyana is being selected to be a part of Guyana's first Mass Games in 1980.

What has been your greatest achievement or proudest moment?
My greatest achievement is putting my three children and myself through college as a single parent, while achieving my life-long dream of becoming a successful fashion designer and business owner.

What words of advice would you give to other Guyanese women?
My words of advice to another Guyanese woman is to look deep within herself, find that one skill that she is most passionate about, understand that is her gift, work hard to develop and master her craft, and trust God every step of the way. Most importantly, use that God-given talent to be a blessing to not only herself, but also to others, while not compromising her moral values

Current Location: Guyana

What is your earliest/most significant memory of Guyana?

When Mr. David Granger was appointed President of Guyana.

What has been your greatest achievement or proudest moment?

My most proud moments were the birth of my two sons.

What words of advice would you give to other Guyanese women?

To be strong, lift your heads high,educate yourselves and stay motivated.

Marcia Mingo

Current location: United States

What is your earliest/most significant memory of Guyana?
Just enjoying simple like connecting with my peers and having fun without the distraction of technology. Wow I really appreciate those moments

What has been your greatest achievement or proudest moment?
Choosing my career field since it gives me the opportunity to save lives daily, I find that most rewarding.

What words of advice would you give to other Guyanese women?
Always believe in yourself.

Carol Cort

Current location: United States

What is your earliest/most significant memory of Guyana?
My most significant memory of Guyana is when the merger
of BHS and QC took place. I was one of the first girls to
enter QC.

**What has been your greatest achievement or proudest
moment?**
My greatest achievement so far has been finding myself
and returning to college after a Workers Comp issue. I
picked up the pieces and changed my career in my thirties
via a BS/MS and I have a supportive partner.

**What words of advice would you give to other Guyanese
women?**
The advice that I would give to other Guyanese women is
no matter what is happening in your life, once you are not
bedridden get educated. Education is a daily lesson not
just a CV(resume). Be determine d and committed to your
goals. Ups and downs don't matter. We overcome.

Holly Williams

Born: Guyana

Current location: Trinidad

What is your earliest/most significant memory of Guyana?
My school days.

What has been your greatest achievement or proudest moment?
My sons.

What words of advice would you give to other Guyanese women?
Be proud of who you are, be confident, work hard and be the best you can.

Marion Shepherd
Born: Guyana
Current location: Guyana

What is your earliest/most significant memory of Guyana?
Going to Kimbia in 1977 for the Guyana National Service.

What has been your greatest achievement or proudest moment?
Joining the Guyana Women's Mining Organisation to help women.

What words of advice would you give to other Guyanese women?
To be a Proverbs 31 woman "Be a virtuous woman" have self-worth and a woman of strength"

Joella Lupe-Grant

Born: London

Current location: London

What is your earliest/most significant memory of Guyana?
Playing Mass Games in the National Park

What has been your greatest achievement or proudest moment?
Organising a Book fund and donating books to Guyana National Library

What words of advice would you give to other Guyanese women?
Be the possibility of fun, loving, unleashed and unstoppable

Words of Inspiration

Love Yourself

Look within
Or you'll be left without
Without your self worth
Fighting self doubt

The answers you want
Lie deep in your heart
Build inner strength
It will set you apart

Seek not from others
Adoration and praise
Learn to self-love
and your standards will raise

Accept nought but the best
Take it from me
You deserve all the world
That's how it should be

The Return

Coming back from the edge
Is one of the hardest things
Like jumping through hoops
Emotional rings

The ties that bind us
To things gone wrong
That stop us savouring
A beautiful song

Life is a song
Melodic and sweet
Look up at the sun
And feel the heat

Savour the moment
Erase all the pain
You have nothing to lose
And a world to gain

Our Collective Power

She stands up straight
Like a coconut tree
Signifying all
That's you and that's me

A woman of substance
She's more than a queen
She knows where we are going
And where we've been

Together we rise
From the dust and the dirt
Women of Kaieteur
Healing the hurt

So, join our group
Be part of it all
Sign up as a member
Don't ignore our call

Kaieteur

We borrowed your name
Because we admired your might
You're revered and regaled
Though out of our sight

Your reputation for power
Is known far and wide
Your unrivalled beauty
Stops people in stride

You epitomise all
That we hope to be
Our strength and our beauty
Is what others should see

Together we revel
In using your name
Increasing your impact
And bringing you fame

Women of Kaieteur is a Global Empowerment Network for Guyanese women and girls. We work on three principles:

Inspiration - Empowerment - Motivation

Borne of the need to do more to progress gender equality in Guyana a few passionate women and men started a series of conversations aimed at developing a vehicle to effect change in Guyana and beyond.

We want to create and build networks with Guyanese women across the globe, encouraging them to share their skills and experiences to positively impact and unlock the potential of women and girls in Guyana.

We know that improved opportunities and outcomes for women have a positive impact on the economy and society as a whole and we believe that it isn't just about the women. We want to collaborate with and educate men about the importance of gender equality.

Women of Kaieteur is a not-for-profit organisation focused the personal and professional development of Guyanese Women and Girls through Empowerment, Inspiration and Motivation. Our mission is to deliver these three themes by galvanising the collective skills and talents of Guyanese women globally to effect positive gender equality changes in Guyana.

For more information go to www.womenofkaieteur.org
Email womenofkaieteur@gmail.com
Twitter: @womenofkaieteur
Facebook: Women of Kaieteur

ABOUT THE PUBLISHER

Welcome to the world of RHJ Publishing. Although conceptualised in 2006, the brand was formally launched in May 2016 in tribute to the late Roydon Haigh Josiah.

Our name reflects the rich ancestry of our founders and enables us to share

HIStory and HERstory

The stories that we share come in all shapes and sizes and we celebrate the eclectic mix of voices and mediums that we use.

We work both formally and informally with writers and creatives to tell their stories and find the best way to share their craft.

We also take great pleasure in working with the next generation of writers by mentoring, supporting and empowering EVERYONE to find their voice.

Our primary distributor is ROI Jelly Ltd, who we work closely with to bring our products to market.

Get involved and have your say:

@RoianneNedd   (Editor)

@RHJPublishing   (Publisher)

Email roijelly@outlook.com for further information

RHJ Publishing is a brand of ROI Jelly Ltd